EMOTIONAL SOBRIETY

Feel-Good Secrets for Everyone

Richard Parenti

BALBOA.
PRESS
A DIVISION OF HAY HOUSE

The author does not speak for Alcoholics Anonymous, nor is Alcoholics Anonymous affiliated in any way with this publication, nor does the author claim that someone else will experience the zone as he has or experience being recovered, feeling good, and growing the way he has by doing steps ten and eleven from the big book of Alcoholics Anonymous as he has restructured them in this book.

Balboa Press books may be ordered through booksellers or by contacting:

Balboa Press
A Division of Hay House
1663 Liberty Drive
Bloomington, IN 47403
www.balboapress.com
1-(877) 407-4847

The author of this book does not dispense medical advice or prescribe the use of any technique as a form of treatment for physical, emotional, or medical problems without the advice of a physician, either directly or indirectly. The intent of the author is only to offer information of a general nature to help you in your quest for emotional and spiritual well-being. In the event you use any of the information in this book for yourself, which is your constitutional right, the author and the publisher assume no responsibility for your actions.

Printed in the United States of America.

ISBN: 978-1-4525-8004-3 (sc)
ISBN: 978-1-4525-8005-0 (e)
Library of Congress Control Number: 2013914864
Balboa Press rev. date: 09/04/2013

This book is dedicated to Ron Lucia, my drinking partner and my one and only friend on the day I quit drinking on January 3, 1974. One year after he told me I was an alcoholic, he died from alcohol poisoning.

Table of Contents

Acknowledgments

THE VISION OF ALWAYS REACHING for the next best-feeling thought is a synthesis of the ideas of my teachers, especially Swami Paramahansa Yogananda, Abraham, Swami Veda Bharati, and Walt Baptiste. This book bears the imprint of those who demonstrated to me what it means to be successful, have fun, and be happy: Lorenzo Walters, Lucy Parker, Mark Wilson, Dr. M. Geddawi, and Donna Patton. I must also acknowledge Linda Macy, Jason Ghent, Alejandro Sabre, and Roger Rauch for their encouragement and support. Finally, I so very much appreciate my dear friend Anna-Mae Mothershed for the many hours she contributed to reading and critiquing the manuscript.

Introduction

I REMINISCED, THINKING, *I AM three months without a drink or a drug*, as I crossed the street of Third Avenue and East 77th Street in New York City, reminding myself that today was March 3, 1974. There was a bounce in my step as I pondered what my next move would be now that I had quit drinking when a brilliant, scintillating white light the size of a basketball entered my stomach from the outside, revolving, twirling and swirling, dazzling me with its brilliance. Then another light illuminated inside my head, a beautiful, sparkling white light the size of a softball. Yet another beam of light streamed up my spine from the light in my stomach to the light in my head, and it exploded within my entire body, which was now bathed in this blinding white light. I felt as though I had entered a zone, a place of immense joy reserved only for the gods.

There I was crossing the street feeling dumbfounded, washed by light and pounded by rolling thunder bursting throughout my body. The joy was indescribable. It was like having an orgasm, but intensified ten million times. The world stood still. My mind went silent. My body shuddered with bliss overflowing from every cell. I couldn't believe it. It was beyond awesome! It was indefinable.

Dazed and delirious, with pleasure pulsating throughout my body, I called my ex-wife, Gail, and told her what happened. She shrieked, "You're nuts!" and slammed down the receiver.

This was my first of many spiritual experiences with the zone. It motivated me to prove to myself that this zone of feeling good without alcohol was not a fluke, but true and reproducible.

Why did I drink? I drank to feel good, and eventually I developed an obsession and didn't know how to stop. When my one and only friend, Ron, told me I was an alcoholic, I quit that very same day. That was January 3, 1974.

The system I formulated involves redoing steps ten and eleven, considered the growth steps, from the big book of Alcoholic Anonymous in a slightly different way, following the leading edge of thought: the conscious use of the mind directed to create a state of consciousness of feeling good, with a specific focus on all that is good about one's self. I firmly believe that we all have complete control over the ability to direct our minds and emotions.

Until I started to do steps ten and eleven in a new way, I was caught in the spider web of recovery by following the twelve steps as outlined in the big book of Alcoholics Anonymous, which can be found in the appendix.[1] Steps ten and eleven kept me in an endless loop of recovery with no way out. But being recovered was an emotional experience that took place within me on a quiet afternoon.

My process began when I heard a dear friend of mine use the word *recovered*. I asked what she meant by it, and she adroitly pointed me to one passage on page 29 in the big book of Alcoholics Anonymous: "Clear cut directions are given showing how we *recovered*." Given this revelation, I was surprised I had never thought through the word *recovered* even though it is mentioned in the big book of Alcoholics Anonymous several times. Instead, I thought I would be in recovery the rest of my life because that was what my sponsor told me.

Later that day, I had an emotional moment of insight while I was sitting in a sidewalk café sipping a latte. It occurred to me that she was right—I was *recovered*.

It was a major insight and impetus to my spiritual growth, as I realized that every time I said, "I am an alcoholic," I was reminding myself of my unworthiness and all the problems I had created in my life. Yet when I said, "I am a *recovered* alcoholic," I intuitively knew I was exercising a new mental muscle that made me feel better about myself. I was thrilled with this new discovery.

I also realized that when using the word *recovered* while still doing steps ten and eleven the way they were written in the big book of Alcoholics Anonymous, my focus remained on my shortcomings instead of on the positive aspects of my character and my recovery.

Finally, I asked God for guidance on how I could change my focus to start feeling good about me, appreciate who I had become over these many years of sobriety, and appreciate who I was in the process of becoming since I had started using the word *recovered* in 2008.

In a meditation, my intuition guided me to redo steps ten and eleven in the manner I will outline in the following chapters and to ask myself empowering questions that reminded me how much I appreciate myself, my world, and other people.

Doing the steps this new way gave me the understanding I needed to make the process of growth fun by focusing on feeling good and recognizing what's right with me.

What does feeling good and feeling bad indicate? Feeling bad indicates my thoughts are negative, and feeling good indicates my thoughts are positive. For example, I know that when I am angry, I feel bad. And I know that when I am happy, I feel good. So when I feel angry or happy, I simply note that I am feeling bad or that I am feeling good. It is that simple.

When I'm feeling bad, I can make a choice and reach for the next best-feeling thought until I feel good, and when I'm feeling good, I can nurture this state with more good-feeling thoughts. The other alternative is to stay stuck in bad feelings. The choice is mine.

When five years ago I had cancer, my negative thoughts of fear led me to a deep, dark, depressed hole for about a year. Then one day I realized that it's time to think differently; when I said that out loud, I knew I had the power of choice. I could choose to continue the downward cycle of thinking thoughts that made me feel afraid and depressed, or I could choose the upward cycle of thinking thoughts that made me feel good.

So from fear I chose to be angry, from anger I chose to be frustrated, and from frustration I chose to feel okay until I got to the point where I said, "If this is the end, let it be." When I reached that point, I laughed like hell. And I felt good, damn good.

In private conversations, people often ask me, "How could you feel good when you were sick with cancer, refused chemotherapy and radiation, and risked that the cancer would come back?" My answer is always the same. I trust my decision, and anytime fear or worry creeps in; I reach for the next best-feeling thought. This line of thinking is working quite well for me.

These private conversations with others inspired me to write this book. I wanted to make this information available to more people, alcoholics and nonalcoholics, everyday people who can benefit from the simple tools I discovered. It's my way of helping others uplift themselves on their quests to feel good about themselves.

This book is not meant for everyone. It is written for those adventurous, brave souls who have an open mind and are willing and ready to embrace feeling good.

I have purposely repeated several statements, themes, and questions throughout the book in order to emphasize a point so that it will be etched in your memory.

My wish for you is that you will have as much fun finding what you are looking for in this book as I had in writing it. Ultimately I hope you will feel good.

I am sure you will.

CHAPTER

1

What Is Emotional Sobriety?

WOKE UP LYING IN my vomit and smelling like a cesspool while an old mangy black dog with a bald face, deformed legs, and a stringy tail stared at me with red crazed eyes. As I peered through the swollen slits of my bloodshot eyes, I thought, *The hell with the dog. Where am I?* Then I remembered: I was nineteen years old, in the Marine Corps, attached to the American Embassy in Vientiane, Laos. The year was 1960. I was lying on the ground in a ditch after a night of drunken debauchery. The city was surrounded by fighters called the Pathet Lao, equivalent to the Vietcong in Vietnam, and I was sure I would be dead by year's end. After all, the Army Colonel Attaché at the American Embassy implied as much at our weekly briefings. "Play hard. Work hard. You never know what will happen next; you could be dead tomorrow." My mission, as part of a ten-man Marine Security Guard unit attached to the State Department in Vientiane, was to provide security to the American Embassy and to the Ambassador. My epitaph would read: "Here lies Richard, a drunkard, who woke up every morning smelling like a sewer and died crying in his beer wondering, 'What's it all about, Alfie?'"

But the gods were of another opinion. Happily, I have *recovered* from a seemingly hopeless state of mind and body that once upon a time was induced by alcohol abuse. My mind is no longer hopeless or a place to be feared, but a delightful place to be revered and honored as it has evolved into a most beautiful thing to explore and direct.

At one time in my life, I felt emptiness deep inside me, along with a sense of hopelessness, which I tried to drown out with alcohol and drugs. Time has proven to me that this state can change. All one has to do is make the decision to give up drinking and drugs and be willing to get well like I did in 1974.

But it wasn't until 2010, two years after I started saying I am a *recovered* alcoholic that I started to rewrite and apply steps ten and eleven in a new way. I became more and more aware that the way I had been doing these two steps since 1974 hindered my growth. The steps produced feelings of unworthiness, instead of feelings of happiness and joy, although they are considered the growth steps to maturity and emotional sobriety. I chose to write about these two steps, because, in my opinion, they can be the core to a person's state of feeling good, but they fail to generate that feeling, if followed as described in the big book of Alcoholics Anonymous.

Step ten says, "Continued to take personal inventory and when we were wrong promptly admitted it."[2] The essence of step ten is that one should "continue to watch for selfishness, dishonesty, resentment, and fear."[3] We are to set right any new blunders as we go through our day. This keeps the focus on what's wrong with a person instead of what's right.

Step eleven says, "Sought through prayer and meditation to improve our conscious contact with God *as we understood Him*, praying only for knowledge of His will for us and the power to carry that out."[4] It also states, "When we retire at night, we constructively review our day. Were we resentful, selfish, dishonest, or afraid? Do we owe an apology?"[5] It suggests that upon awakening we ask God for guidance, and as we go through our day we ask God for direction, inspiration, an intuitive thought, or assistance. While the essence of step eleven to make conscious contact and ask God for guidance is commendable, the directions, except for the prayers, in step eleven, just like step ten, reinforce what's wrong with a person instead of what's right.

I modified these two steps in a way that would allow me to recapture the state of feeling good I experienced when I was in the zone. So today, when people ask if I am an alcoholic, I always answer, "I am a *recovered* alcoholic." This is only a slight but very powerful variation of the phrase "I am an alcoholic."

According to the big book of Alcoholics Anonymous, *recovered* means, "We have *recovered* from a hopeless condition of mind and body."[6] When I say that, I often get a scowl from others that tells me that secretly they

3

are thinking I am a jerk. I know that because I have been told by others how arrogant and egotistic that sounds to them. Apparently they feel I lack humbleness. I find their comments amusing and entertaining, because I truly have found emotional sobriety.

So what is emotional sobriety? I believe it is the full understanding, recognition, and awareness that one has *recovered* from a seemingly hopeless state of mind and body, has solved one's drinking problem, and is a miracle of mental health.

Once *recovered*, one is able to live a fully productive, happy life without beating oneself up over and over, as so many people do by reminding themselves, "I am an alcoholic." For this implies that one is still struggling with alcoholism, still labeling oneself with a disease, and identifying with one's character defects that must be wrestled to the ground day by day, week by week. I was no different until I realized that I had *recovered*.

Recovered in its broadest sense implies that I am healthy again, moving with the flow of life, enjoying it, and accepting myself and others where we are in the moment, while willingly and happily continuing to grow and change as a cooperative component to all things I want.

Prior to this awakening, I was a loner, an angry young man running on fear. I kept reinforcing this concept of myself as I followed the directions of step ten and step eleven as they are written in the big book of Alcoholics Anonymous.

Now my life has changed. I set a sterling example of what it means to be mentally and emotionally healthy. I tested this new method on myself for six months, and have since mentored nine people in my interpretation of the two steps. I am happy to report that it is leading them to their own realization of recovery, healing, and happiness.

One of the people I mentor, Jack, says, "In one year this new system has changed my perspective of my wife, and my relationship with her has gotten better and better and better. And that's a miracle, because for the last three years we've been fighting almost nonstop every day, like two junkyard dogs fighting over the same bone."[7]

Another person I mentor, Jane, says, "This has been a lifesaver. I thought there was something terribly wrong with me, because when I was doing steps ten and eleven, I was constantly reminded of my character defects. I no longer do that and I feel much better."[8]

And yet another person I mentor, Paul, states, "Since I've started these two steps, I can tell you my attitude is extremely positive, and I am now feeling good most of the time about who I am for the first time in more years than I want to remember."[9]

And last, Gertrude, says, "I am so happy you showed me this new approach. When you asked me if I go around introducing myself when I'm feeling good—'Hi, my name is Gertrude and I'm depressed'—you made me laugh and I understood immediately what you meant by the use of the word *recovered*."[10]

"*Recovered*" is a feel-good word in my experience and in the experience of others that I mentor.

C H A P T E R

2

The Law of Attraction

REMEMBER SITTING ON A park bench in New York's Central Park in early 1975 when I thought back to the past year and asked myself how I had ended up there. My wife had divorced me unexpectedly, I was being sued, my car had been repossessed, I had only fifty dollars in my pocket, had been thrown out of my house, and had just gotten fired. To top it all off, I had just been told that I was an alcoholic.

As I sat there, unexpectedly and suddenly, the same happy feeling I had had the year prior returned. This time I felt a deep calm and heightened awareness. My thoughts stopped. It was as though time stood still and everything moved in slow motion.

Then a very authoritative voice spoke: "The law of attraction states that energy follows thought and returns to its source, which in this case is you, the map-maker. In other words, based on your thinking and feeling, you have attracted what you are currently experiencing, whether you are aware of your thoughts and feelings or not. You created it all; everything that has happened to you happened as a result of your thoughts. Your alcoholism was only a symptom. Your negative thinking generated negative feelings, which created negative circumstances. There is no fine print to this statement. If you want to get well, change your thinking!"

I sat there, dumbfounded. Was this God? Who knew? Who cared? I felt joyful, and in that moment of joy, I realized that all my restless thoughts, my arguments with my wife, and my irresponsible negative thinking resulted in our divorce, my car being reposed, and me getting fired. It was as if I had been hit with a thunderbolt of truth, and I knew it. Just like when Ron said that I was an alcoholic, I got it immediately.

Then, this same voice reminded me that good things had happened in my life, too, and to go back to 1955 and begin there to connect my thoughts to what manifested for me.

As I reflected, I remembered that, in 1955, I had wished someone would give me a car. I made this wish when I was feeling good. Over the next thirty years, six cars were given to me free and clear. In 1965, I thought positively that I would love to live in Europe and work in the field of international relations. Then I forgot about that thought. In 1967, I was offered a job in naval intelligence in Europe. The thought had come true. Years later I thought how much fun it would be to own a restaurant in Europe. In 1977, I was offered to take over a restaurant free of charge on the island of Ibiza, Spain, with the stipulation that I would share the profits with the landlord at the end of the tourist season. Again, the thought had come true.

I have had several more experiences just like these, which demonstrated to me that the law of attraction was a reality in my life. I reasoned that certain thoughts came true, if they were stated as specific intentions of something I wanted to experience, and if I gave plenty of energy into thinking about them while in a feel-good state.

Then, there were those thoughts that never came true, because they had no emotional juice behind them. In other words, I really didn't give a damn if they manifested; therefore, they didn't.

And then, there were many negative thoughts that came true and led to unwanted experiences. Such as the time I was angry with a coworker for skimming money; the next thing I knew, she told the owner it was me. I got fired. I never connected the dots. Once I was mad at my wife and went to work fuming, and this time a Jeep Cherokee broadsided me. Again, I was unable to see how my anger had created the car accident, but it did. Then there was the time my friend, Jim, got so angry with his wife that he had a heart attack. Luckily, he lived to tell the tale. Before the argument, he told me that he was mad that his wife, Jennifer, had taken one thousand dollars out of the account without his knowledge. As he relived this in his mind, thinking that she was selfish, he got angrier and angrier until he exploded when he confronted her, and wound up in the emergency room.

In the context of recovery, I realize that happy thoughts generate more happy thoughts, and negative thoughts generate more negative thoughts. So when I say I am *recovered*, I generate more happy thoughts that remind me of all the good inside me. And when I say I am an alcoholic, I generate more negative thoughts that remind me of my faults and the shame and guilt I carry with me around my drinking.

I know now that when I launch a missile of desire from either a place of conscious desire of something I want or from a place of conscious desire of something that I don't want, it will manifest if I give enough energy to the thought, be it negative or positive.

I have proven to myself that a person's thoughts attract what they want based on how they feel (feel good) or create unwanted experiences based on how they feel (feel bad).

Examples:

- Conscious desire of something you want: "I want perfect health." This is a conscious desire of what I want. Sometimes it is good to be specific and other times it is not. In this case, since I don't know what perfect health is, I leave that up to the gods to figure out.
- Conscious desire of something you don't want: "I'm fearful because I have an irregular heartbeat." This thought, depending on the strength of the thought, creates more negative thoughts and

feelings. For example, when I had cancer, the more I thought about it, the more fearful and depressed I became, the less people wanted to be around me, and the less I wanted to be around them, when in fact I secretly wished people would be around me more often to comfort me.

In other words, when I say yes to something, I draw something I want into my experience, and when I say no to something, I magnetize something I don't want and bring it into my experience.

My experience tells me that all things that occur in my life come to me by my request in my thoughts and feelings. You may disagree with that, because you want to avoid responsibility for how you think, feel, and act. Or perhaps you prefer to blame your situation on karma or some other excuse so you can weasel out of being held accountable.

Early in sobriety, I sponsored a young man who, charged with robbery with a gun, had spent time in Attica state prison for his crime. One day he told me that he always knew who to rob. He could smell people's fear, and they'd become his target. The smell, he said, was in the way they walked, hunched over, the way they avoided looking him in the eyes. He said that he could hear them silently saying to him, "It's not safe to walk the streets of New York at three in the morning." He knew then that would be his victim.

Based on what I was told by this incredible, authoritative, and loving voice as well as on my personal experiences, I can only say that I have been a victim of my own thoughts.

My encounter with this voice also demonstrated to me that within me is a place of calm, a place of deep silence without rambling thoughts, a place of endless joy bubbling up without any outside stimuli; it is a place where the word *recovered* becomes unquestionable and my experience tells me it's a natural state of being. I call this place the zone.

I believe our most important work is to get into the zone where it feels good. By being in the zone, I align myself with who I really am. I do that by directing my thoughts.

A thought is a vibration. A feeling is a vibration. Combining the two, in my humble opinion, is how you attract things to you. Think fearful thoughts and attract fearful, unwanted experiences. Think happy thoughts and attract happy, wanted experiences.

Last night, I was having dinner with Barbara, a close lady friend who shares my quest for feeling good, at an upscale restaurant in Modesto, California. I was telling her that my desire with this book was to help as many people as possible. The gentleman sitting to my left interrupted me and asked what the book was about. I explained. He said, "I am interested because I am in the self-help book business in Canada, and would like to see a finished copy and see what I can do to help you market it in Canada."

I also discovered one can delay stuff from manifesting by looking for the evidence of it or by feeling negative in general. In other words, I remember thinking about having a loving relationship with someone, a positive thought, only to be afraid of being rejected the next moment, a negative thought.

The strongest thought was the fear of being rejected. Every time I thought about the relationship I wanted, I was thinking negative thoughts reminding me that there was no reason for the relationship to work, until I finally learned to distract myself from needing evidence that something would work. Instead, I'd focus my attention on feeling good by reviewing what I wanted when in a feel-good state.

I'd say things like, "My life is unfolding perfectly," or "I love feeling good because it feels good to feel good." I'd also reaffirm that what I want is being brought to me by the law of attraction.

I keep my attention away from looking for evidence, as I am happy with the idea of having what I want. Evidence is great when it happens, but when I worry about the evidence, I know I am delaying the manifestation of what I want.

I believe you block what's coming to you when you are critical about someone, when you are condemning the rich, when you are complaining about the government, when you are complaining about our current medical system; in short, you block what's coming to you when you are too critical.

I learned this in my own life by noticing how slowly money came into my life, how problems with the government came to me unannounced, and how many things that I wanted seemed to take forever to manifest. For example, for as long as I can remember, I complained about western medicine. Every time I went to the doctor, my experience was less than satisfying and incredibly expensive, until I began to appreciate western medicine and all the good they do for people and for me. Over the years, I have noticed that my experiences are more pleasant, enjoyable, and less expensive.

My experience also tells me that the journey to the zone—where I believe that Source Energy, God, exists—is the real fun stuff. My revisions of steps ten and eleven are about just that: keeping focused on feeling good and getting into the zone.

On page 164 of the big book of Alcoholics Anonymous, it states, "We realize we know only a little. God will constantly disclose more to you and to us." And God has disclosed to me how to handle these growth steps ten and eleven in a fun, harmonious way in line with my expansion and growth, freeing me from my previous negative focus. This was disclosed to me in a meditation.

This does not mean that I ignore my feelings when I feel bad. Instead, I embrace the negative feelings, acknowledge them, and turn my attention to reaching for the next best-feeling thought that's available to me until I feel good, no matter how long it takes. Along the way, I ask questions like: What can I learn from this? What's good about this?

Take, for example, my irregular heartbeat. When my heart goes haywire, what could possibly be good? Simple: I get to rest and reflect on what an amazing life I have been living and on the many wonderful people who have been in my life. I am so blessed.

Or what can I learn from cancer? I faced my fear of death and said to God, "If it's my time to go, let's get the show on the road. In the meantime, I am going to have fun and enjoy my life."

The law of attraction taught me that by beating the drum that says, "I'm an alcoholic," and doing the growth steps ten and eleven as outlined in the big book of Alcoholics Anonymous, I continued to beat myself up emotionally and attract more negative thoughts and feelings, which in turn continually led me to feeling depressed and anxious.

Look around you! It doesn't take genius to figure out that the predominant emotional state of most people on this planet is negative. And from this negative mind-set, one always attracts more negative thoughts and more negative experiences.

Common negative themes in our society regarding relationships, medicine, business, careers, money, religion, and more express themselves in common phrases such as the following: What's wrong with this picture? What am I, chopped liver? I'm a good person. Why is this happening to me? All businesses care about are profit and screw the common man. Government doesn't care for anything except itself. I don't know why I even vote anymore as all politicians are crooks. How do I know a politician is lying when he opens his mouth? The rich get all the tax breaks and keep getting richer, while I work hard and pay more and more taxes. It's not fair, I tell you.

My experience has shown me that these thought patterns attract more negative thoughts until one feels angry, irritable, or depressed. But again, one must examine one's thoughts and connect them to what they are experiencing.

How do these negative thought patterns influence our lives? Just ask yourself how much fun is it to be around a negative person, and you'll have your answer.

Do steps ten and eleven as outlined in this book and you will go a long way in nurturing and developing a positive mental attitude and feeling good about yourself. In addition, keep a diary, and at the top of each page, write down names of people, including yourself, and institutions. Underneath each name or institution, write a list of all their positive aspects, and review this list often to add to it whenever you can.

Accept where you are and move on from there. If you don't recognize and accept where you are at the moment, you cannot move forward.

Once I was homeless. Then I moved into a dingy hotel room. From there, I got a studio apartment. From there, I moved onto a fifty-foot yacht in Cabo San Lucas, Mexico. I acknowledged where I was in each stage, appreciating where I was and reminding myself that I was in the process of living a higher quality life. And I did.

Self-appreciation is a major doorway to allowing the law of attraction to bring to you all the things that you want. From now on, make it a point to appreciate yourself and other people, and learn to value their opinions as well as your own.

There is much freedom in doing this. Don't take my word for it. Prove it to yourself by doing it. One day I was listening to a group of alcoholics. As I listened, I reminded myself that I am who I am and that I am pleased with it, joyful about it. The other person is who he or she is, which is different than me, but it is also good. I am perfectly okay with the way other people are. They have their game plan and I have mine. God bless them, I wish them the best. Every time I do this, I feel a sense of peace in my heart and I find myself genuinely appreciating them.

To generate more good feelings, make up feel-good statements or stories that help you create a new you.

Examples:

- From now on, I'm going to hang out with people who are uplifting and positive. For example, I have a friend who has written several books on spiritual growth, another friend who is highly successful in business, and yet another who is a successful artist. What they all have in common is laughter, a positive mental attitude, a zest for life, and a willingness to help one another. Whenever I am around them, I feel uplifted.

- I'm going to feel less responsible for other people. Sometimes I run across people who are broke and begging. I used to feel I had to give them money every time they asked, but not anymore, as I can feel for them without the need to fix them.

- I came to this planet to play, to have fun, to expand, to experience life to its fullest while being carefree and loving. Sometimes I'll just get in my car and take a drive in the country, or I'll take a walk because it feels good to me to walk.

- I've decided to pamper myself. So I go to the spa monthly and treat myself to a facial and a massage.
- I like making decisions that make me feel good. Just the other day, I decided to treat myself to a vanilla ice cream cone. That felt great, since I hadn't had one in months.
- I occasionally go to an afternoon movie by myself. This is such a simple pleasure that sometimes I wonder why I don't do it more often.

The law of attraction is the guts of what makes steps ten and eleven yield more positive, promising results. One conscious positive thought can lead to more feel-good thoughts that can take you into the zone. But don't take my word for it. Put the law of attraction to the test and find out for yourself.

C H A P T E R

3

What Is the Zone?

F OR ME, THE ZONE IS a place of indescribable happiness and freedom from within, experienced without any outside stimuli. It is a place so soothing and comforting that everything else becomes irrelevant. It is truly a feel-good zone with many different levels.

Before I discovered the zone, my thoughts aimlessly drifted, or so I thought, until I learned about the law of attraction. Now I know I can use my mind and get in the zone by directing my thoughts purposely.

I found that feeling good leads to the deeper levels—the feelings of deep calm, indescribable joy, and unfathomable silence bubbling up endlessly from within. When I am in these states, I find myself having to remain quiet. To me, the zone represents the doorway to Infinity, but it is up to us to prove that for ourselves.

I find I can be in the zone feeling good, knocking on the door to Infinity while driving somewhere, talking to someone, taking a walk, having coffee in a sidewalk café at the same time, or I can be in the zone in a quiet meditative state at home in a chair with my eyes closed. When I find myself roaming the deeper levels of the zone, the best I can do is just sit.

You might be asking right about now why you should get in the zone. Simple, I get into the zone to feel good and align with my true nature. I'd rather feel good than bad. Besides, I feel like I am a beacon for people who want to feel better. What about you? How do you want to feel?

The zone is what I believe Bill Wilson, cofounder of Alcoholics Anonymous, was referring to on page 133 of the big book of Alcoholics Anonymous. "We are sure God wants us to be happy, joyous, and free."[11] I often feel like that when I'm in the zone.

In Bill Wilson's article, "The Next Frontier: Emotional Sobriety," written in 1953 and published in *Grapevine Magazine* in 1958, he states, "I think that many oldsters who have put our AA 'booze cure' to severe but successful tests still find they often lack emotional sobriety. Perhaps they will be the spearhead for the next major development in AA—the development of much more real maturity and balance (which is to say, humility) in our relations with ourselves, with our fellows, and with God."[12]

Later in the article he says, "I found I had to exert every ounce of will and action to cut off these faulty emotional dependencies upon people, upon AA, indeed, upon any set of circumstances whatsoever."[13]

I believe that his definition of emotional sobriety is to shift our focus from dependence on outside sources and things to inside and on God. This is my interpretation, and it is reflected particularly in steps ten and eleven.

My new interpretation does not keep me from mentoring people on how to do the steps according to the big book of Alcoholics Anonymous. In fact, I instruct newcomers how to do the twelve steps as taught to me. However, when we get to steps ten and eleven, I show them both: how to do them according to the directions in the big book of Alcoholics Anonymous, and how to do them as I've outlined here. It's their choice which way they want to proceed, the traditional way or my way.

I am convinced that as you grow you will feel and know you have *recovered*; you will experience that emotional moment of awareness. You will find your own way of doing the steps anew, following your own inner guidance as I have followed mine. You will also find tremendous appreciation for the original twelve steps.

At some point in my sobriety, as I reflected back upon my earlier experiences in New York City, I realized that because of these experiences, I eventually began seeking ways to get into the zone within and keep myself going in this direction. It always began with meditation.

The emptiness I once felt and tried to fill with alcohol is slowly shrinking. Now, I fill that hole by getting into the zone by using steps ten and eleven as I describe them in this book.

C H A P T E R

4

How to Get into the Zone

KNOW FROM MY EXPERIENCE that the zone is within, and that upon genuinely leaning into or being in the zone, I feel really good. Those whom I have mentored have experienced the zone too, in ways that have brought them feelings of happiness. Larry, a young man I mentor, told me, "From everything I've ever read, I always felt there was a place like the zone within me that would lead me to discover deeper parts of me, only no one ever showed me how to get there. Thank you for taking the time to show me how to get into the zone by my own efforts. I love this feeling of joy that I get when I am in the zone."[14]

So how do I get in the zone?

The following list is but a few of the thousands of different ways to lean into and get into the zone. Some ways require action, others require thinking, and one requires meditating.

- Go from a generally negative to a generally positive dialogue.
- Pet your cat or dog.
- Get a massage.
- Sit quietly and think how wonderful you feel being alive.
- Take a walk in nature.
- Watch funny movies.
- Make positive statements.
- Go dancing.
- Sing.
- Go to the museum.
- Swim.
- Pray.
- Run.
- Sit down and meditate.
- Watch the sunset.
- Enjoy sex.
- Play golf.
- Go horseback riding.
- Play tennis.
- Go skiing.
- Make up stories that make you feel good.

And if nothing on this list works for you, make up your own list.

Let's use the first item on the list. How do I go from a generally negative dialogue to a generally positive dialogue?

Reach for the next best-feeling thought until you feel good, no matter how long that takes.

For example, when my heartbeat becomes irregular (a condition where abnormal electrical activity in my heart causes premature or delayed heartbeats that, if continuous and constant, can lead to cardiac death) and I feel fear, I make my heart health story general, believable, and soothing. The key point is how the story makes me feel by the time I reach the end. My dialogue with myself may go like this as I reach for the next best-feeling thought.

- Well, here I am once again.
- This is frustrating.
- But, it's all right where I am, and there is no wrong in being where I am. I am where I am, and that's enough and I'm okay with that, because I am where I am.
- My history with this condition has shown me it always passes. My heartbeat always goes back to normal, always, and that's a fact.
- I've proven over the years that it's harmless.
- So realizing all this, it's really no big deal. Maybe it's a little tiring, but it's no big deal.
- I feel I am already in the solution, because I realize I am in the process of feeling better every day by my willingness to get into the zone as often as I can, either by way of my thoughts or my actions.
- Sometimes I get kicked out of the zone when this health issue gets activated or when I falsely

focus on worry or fear, which I am in the process of changing now.

- I realize that it's the journey of reaching for the next best-feeling thought that is my reward, not the destination. I sometimes forget that.
- So what is my final destination? Simply, it is feeling happy and joyous no matter what is going on with my health, and being free from my current worried emotional response to my health issue. When that changes, my vibration changes, and when that changes, my health changes.
- Yes, I am willing to feel the ease of well-being.
- I'm sure there are people who feel well-being although in the past they felt like I do right now.
- In fact, I've talked to a woman who had the same health issue and is fine now.
- And there are probably a lot more people like her who have worked their way out of the way I feel and are experiencing their well-being as well.
- Just by reaching for the next best-feeling thought I get into the process of moving downstream with the current to a better feeling place and I like that.
- I truly believe and expect that there will come a time I will reap the benefits of this way of thinking, and I will give thanks for these stressful times that I have had.
- All right, let's get the show on the road. Smile, Richard.

This is my story regarding my irregular heartbeat. It is only intended to demonstrate how to reach for the next best-feeling thought until you feel better. Use this as your guide and insert your own words. And remember, make it believable and soothing.

What I learned is that thinking positive thoughts while awake, using a story like this, led me to lean into the zone and put me in a positive mental state.

Knowing why you want to get in the zone is the starting point of getting in. So why bother getting into the zone? Using a story like the above helped me generate good feelings and assisted me to lean into the zone. Remember thoughts generate feelings, and positive feelings lead you to the zone.

So get out a piece of paper and write down your reasons for getting in the zone. Here are some examples that help me:

- I'm getting into the zone because it feels good there.
- I'm getting into the zone because I feel playful there.
- Bottom line, I am getting into the zone because it feels good to feel good.

I explain how to use steps ten and eleven in a new innovative way, how to generate feeling good, how to get into the zone, and how to milk the zone by staying in it for as long as possible. When in it, just enjoy that state of awareness of feeling good.

What do I do when I am in the zone? I nurture this good feeling by pondering questions like: What do I like about me? What's good about life, about government, about business? And as I am getting my answers, I go about my daily life if I am in public, or, if I am sitting down somewhere, I just sit and take pleasure in this state of good feeling. I always remind myself of my dominant intention to feel good, to please me, to be good to me.

In other words, I exercise this mental muscle of feeling good, no matter what I am doing and as often as I can remember to do so. For example, when I wake up in the morning, I sit and meditate to get in the zone. During the day, I remind myself why I like being in the zone. Often, I will go for a drive and tell myself stories that feel good. Sometimes I will go for a walk downtown, appreciating all the things I like about the town. Alternately, I will visit a friend.

One time I was in a good mood visiting my dear friend Stephanie when she said something that was contrary to what I believed. I found myself smiling, feeling good inside, reminding myself she's got her game plan and I've got mine, and it's okay with me that she is the way she is. Besides, I realized that I had no desire to try to change her, as I know only she could do that. Thus I was able to maintain my state of feeling good.

5

Learn to Appreciate
Self and Others

P EOPLE'S ORIGINAL HARDWARE, THEIR ORIGINAL pure mind, is just as pure today as is yours. When we were born, our minds were innocent and pure, and this innocent mind believed what it was told. When growing up, people are filled with information that creates belief systems. I call this the software we express in everyday life through our ego. I realize that when confrontations or disagreements occur, it is always my ego judging another's ego, or my beliefs versus another's beliefs.

I believe understanding this brought forth the process to appreciate and accept myself and others. For me this set the groundwork to being nonjudgmental. It released unconscious guilt and shame, and thus started the process of healing from within, which I believe helped me realize that I was a *recovered* alcoholic.

For me, being nonjudgmental means understanding that everyone is preprogrammed by their genetics and by the context in which they grew up. Everyone grew up in a certain time period and collected data that created the software program (ego and belief systems) that programmed their mind. That data came from parents, culture, peer groups, the movies and TV programs watched, the music listened to, teachers, friends, the conditions in which they were raised, religion, job, bosses, intimate relationships, and life experiences. Such conditioning is responsible for people behaving the way they do.

I was programmed just as other people were programmed. But with awareness and understanding, this changed for me.

As soon as I was willing to eliminate my criticism of others, my judging people, situations, or myself right and wrong, acceptance, compassion, forgiveness, and appreciation became operative words for me.

- Acceptance means allowing people to be where they are and a situation to be the way it is.
- Compassion means being able to see a person's pain and a willingness to recognize and see all things, events, and people, including yourself, as innocent and pure without the need to fix anyone or anything.
- Forgiveness means not passing judgment on another's behavior because you understand and accept that the person cannot say nor do anything

different because of their conditioning. It is what it is. It's that simple.

- Appreciation means valuing something or someone. It is the absence of doubt, fear, worry, anger, hate, blame, and self-pity, and everything that feels bad. It is a feeling of joy without resistance to all things and to all people.

Being judgmental was one of the main ways I kept myself from feeling good. Releasing judgment of other people and events opened the door for me to understand what the word *appreciation* really means and how feeling good feels.

"What is the use of fault-finding, criticizing, and blaming others? It is a disease of the mind that infects everyone. Appreciation is the cure. Accept others as they are."[15]

C H A P T E R

6

Appreciation versus Gratitude

I FOUND THAT APPRECIATION MEANS valuing something or someone. In many cases, it means increasing the value of something, like being a *recovered* alcoholic. Appreciation is a feeling that comes from within. To me true appreciation is a feeling, a highly aware state of mind that feels good.

My personal experience tells me that appreciation in its purest form is pure joy pulsating through me as I am looking at or thinking about someone or something. The other day I was having coffee at Café Bistro when I started reminding myself how much I appreciate that I am a loyal friend, that I am willing to grow and change, that I am open-minded, and that I keep my word. As I continued down this thought pattern of self-appreciation, I entered the zone and stayed there for about forty-five minutes, feeling immense joy as I watched all the people in the café hustle and bustle, while I was in a quiet, calm, awake, and functional state sipping on my coffee.

At some point during these forty-five minutes, I was surprised as I experienced a deeper state of awareness—being connected with what I call Source Energy or God. It lasted about one minute, and tears of joy streamed down my face. I was beyond happy. Then, I calmed down and realized that appreciation at its deepest level leads to being in sync with all of that which I AM.

I discovered that appreciation feels like a state of wholeness, worthiness, wellness, and love.

To me, gratitude is looking at something I've struggled with and have overcome, like my drinking and negative behavior patterns. I am grateful I am not in that struggle anymore. People may think that *appreciation* and *gratitude* are synonyms, but I do not.

When I say I am a grateful alcoholic, I am focusing on all the difficulty, struggle, shame, and guilt I experienced when drinking. In my opinion, the word *grateful* keeps my focus on the hardships I went through to be sober. When I talk about gratitude, I am almost always talking about something I have overcome.

Thus, the alcoholic mind-set and behavior is activated when a person makes the statement, "I am a grateful alcoholic," which keeps the person focused on all the problems of an alcoholic. What they have overcome, they are not completely ready to let go. In my opinion, people are usually grateful for stuff that is not active in their life anymore, but they rattle it around in their thoughts on an unconscious level when using the word *grateful*.

That's my opinion, and based on my experience and definition of *appreciation* and *gratitude*, the two words are remarkably different. The important issue is that I find thoughts that feel good to me, and *appreciation* is certainly a deeper, more pervasive, constructive, positive, and uplifting word than *gratitude*.

When I am chatting to someone who has an alcohol problem, or to someone who has a challenge of any sort, I always remind myself how much I appreciate where they are in their sobriety or in their life, and how much I value their opinion. I am relieved to know that I have the tools to free myself from negative judgment, which evokes in me a state of feeling good, often accompanied by a quiet mind without any editorial comment on anything or anyone.

I am not always free of judgment, but I certainly know when I am not and I know how to change my focus, unless of course I like feeling bad and negative, or I am trying to improve my self-esteem by belittling or judging another. I can remember being like that sometimes throughout my life, yet being unaware of the consequences. In fact, I think I enjoyed being judgmental as it made me feel superior, albeit in a shallow way.

The key to appreciation is to keep my focus on valuing who I am and all the good things that are or will be in my life.

Bottom line, appreciation is a first-class ticket to feeling good and being *recovered.* I am convinced that it is a meaningful way into the zone.

7

How to Do Step Ten and Milk the Zone

THE FIRST PART OF STEP ten says, "Continued to take personal inventory."[16]

This new personal inventory is designed to help you milk the zone. First, tell yourself, "I've got only one thing to do today and that's to feel good, to please myself, to be good to me; everything else flows from that."

This sets the tone to get in the zone and to milk it. Meditating at home, I have been able to be in the zone for about an hour. When I'm out walking around, I can be in the zone for about ten minutes. In a café I can maintain the zone for about an hour. Then, when I remind myself of my intention of feeling good, I just naturally start feeling good and move toward the zone.

In doing my personal inventory, I remind myself as often as I can to talk about what I appreciate about me, about government, about business, about religions, about others.

I also remind myself how it feels to be in the zone, how it feels to be in the process of getting into the zone, all of which leads to feeling good.

I am going to be a bit repetitive here as it is important to realize that by focusing and refocusing upon these statements it will become easier to feel good, move into the zone, and to milk it.

So right now, stop what you are doing, sit down, take out a piece of paper, and complete the following statements. This is the first step in taking your new inventory.

Example: I appreciate all the good government does for people.

- I appreciate . . .
- I appreciate . . .
- I appreciate . . .
- I appreciate . . .
- I appreciate . . .
- I appreciate . . .
- I appreciate . . .
- I appreciate . . .
- I appreciate . . .
- I appreciate . . .

Now use the following statements to milk the zone or make up your own statements that make you feel good.

Examples:

- When I'm in the zone, I feel good.
- When I'm in the zone, I feel whole and complete.
- When I'm in the zone, I feel happy.
- When I'm in the zone, I feel a quiet calm bubbling up inside me.
- When I'm in the zone, I feel uplifted.
- When I'm in the zone, I feel fantastic.
- When I'm in the zone, I feel exceptional.
- When I'm in the zone, I feel at peace.
- When I' m in the zone, I feel worthy.
- When I'm in the zone, I feel energized.
- When I'm in the zone, I feel fulfilled.
- When I'm in the zone, time disappears and satisfaction speeds up.
- When I'm in the zone, I feel powerful.
- When I'm in the zone, I feel joyous.
- When I'm in the zone, I feel happy.
- When I'm in the zone, I feel carefree.
- When I'm in the zone, I feel free.
- When I'm in the zone, I feel elated.
- When I'm in the zone, I feel authentic.
- When I'm in the zone, I feel unlimited.
- When I'm in the zone, I feel unstoppable.
- When I'm in the zone, I feel enriched.
- When I'm in the zone, I feel yummy.
- When I'm in the zone, I feel nonjudgmental.

- When I'm in the zone, I feel on top of the world.
- When I'm in the zone, I feel all is well.

These statements are only suggestions. Their purpose is to create a feeling state within. They have nothing to do with implementing anything. They are about feeling something, not doing something.

Since we are always in the process of thinking something, which is always generating feelings, here are some specific believable statements to further help milk the zone. Again, this is about creating a feeling space within, not about taking action or doing something. The result you are looking for is to feel good. If these examples don't work for you, make up your own.

Examples:

- I'm in the process of feeling good.
- I'm in the process of being happy.
- I'm in the process of having more and more fun in my life.
- I'm in the process of being confident, wise, and compassionate.
- I'm in the process of finding more and more thoughts that make me feel good.
- I'm in the process of loving myself.
- I'm in the process of mastering the art and science of feeling good.

- I'm in the process of understanding and mastering the law of attraction in its entirety.
- I'm in the process of living an amazing life.
- I'm in the process of being in the zone be what matters most to me.
- I'm in the process of mastering my emotions.
- I'm in the process of allowing all that I want into my life.
- I'm in the process of seeing things that make me feel good.

Also, from time to time, I ask empowering questions when I find myself outside the zone feeling neutral or feeling bad. The importance of these questions is for you to discover what your answers are rather than reading about examples from my life experiences. So get out a piece of paper and write down these questions and start answering them as they relate to any specific incident in your life you would like to understand better and grow from.

- What would have been a wiser action?
- What can I learn from this situation?
- What can I learn from or about this person?
- What are the positive aspects of this person, this situation, this event?
- How can I grow from this?
- What do I want to bring into my life?
- What's the next best-feeling thought that will make me feel better?

- What thoughts make me happy?
- What makes me feel good?
- What things do I like to do that make me feel good?

The second part of step ten says, "And when we were wrong promptly admitted it."[17] This means to make amends when wrong.

What is an amend? I was taught that it is setting right a wrong. It is correcting past wrongful behavior. I discovered that this not only relates to people involved in twelve-step programs, but also works for other people from all walks of life. The following experience is universal and applies to alcoholics and non-alcoholics, men and women alike.

For example, when I had an affair, my sponsor asked me if my wife knew and, if she did, how she felt about the affair. I told him she found out and was hurt and mad as hell. He told me to give her a few weeks to cool off, then go and make amends, telling her I was wrong for the hurt I caused her, asking what I could do to set right the wrong.

I followed his advice, because I was told that I would never overcome my alcohol addiction until I did all my amends, including this one. To set right the wrong I caused, I did what he suggested. It was a disaster. It made her cry, hurt her feelings, and made her mad. Our marriage worsened and eventually we divorced.

What did I learn from this? I learned it was important to trust myself and not rely on others to figure out what's good for me.

So I suggest that before making amends, consider the following thoughts:

- When I make amends, am I saying I didn't choose to do whatever I did and that I was not responsible for my behavior or my beliefs, because of my lack of awareness, because of my drug or alcohol abuse, or because someone else made me do it?
- Am I going to make amends hoping I'll feel better when the other person forgives me, so I won't have to admit to myself that I really did what I did and I did it on purpose?
- Since there are no accidents, why do I need to make amends for something I wanted to do and did?
- Am I trying to relieve my conscience of my own shame, stupidity, ignorance, and guilt?
- Why do I want to bring up old stuff that takes me into a negative place and reminds me and the other person of my past hurtful deeds and the pain and hurt I caused them?
- Am I attempting to make myself feel good at the expense of another, because I was told the only way to get well is to make amends?
- Since when am I responsible for the way others feel or for the way they respond to my behavior or my words?

Think on this. In my opinion, God, the Source Energy, sees me as whole, complete, and worthy. So why in the world would I say to God, "Sorry, God, I think you made a mistake, I'm a bad person and a sinner, and I have to make amends to feel better and get your favor?"

Truly, does it make sense to keep digging up the past that forces you and the other person to relive the negativity and the hurt caused by your past words and actions? After what happened in my marriage, I think long and hard before making amends.

Am I implying that you are exempt from making amends? Absolutely not! Rather, my suggestion in making amends is simple. If you owe money, pay it back. If you made a mistake in business or in a personal relationship, ask what would have been a wiser behavior, admit to yourself that you made a mistake, and commit to correcting your thinking and actions. Resolve not to repeat what you said or did. In other words, learn from your experience. However, if, for whatever reason, you still feel you have to make amends, do so by saying something from the heart that will be uplifting and positive for the other person and yourself.

My amends to my wife taught me to stay away from beating myself up over what I did, or bringing up the specifics of what I think I did wrong.

I have made several amends. Some I regretted, as they only made matters worse. For example, I was drinking at work and failed to perform my job adequately, which, over time, cost the company a considerable amount of money. I remember telling the owner I had been drinking on the job, mismanaged the business, causing a decrease in profit, and asking what I could do to make this right. He said, "Simple. Pay me the money that was lost, and get another job."

I discovered that people reacted in five ways to my amends. One, they had no idea what I was talking about. Two, they got mad because they were reminded of a painful experience. Three, they said thanks and asked me to pay what I owed and then leave. Four, they told me they understood I wanted to make amends but it wasn't necessary as they had long ago let go of the incident and moved on. Five, they said thank you and wanted to chat and find out what had created this change in me. I felt their sincerity.

From my experience, I found it beneficial to make amends short, sweet, and uplifting, no more than five minutes. If you cannot be encouraging, supportive, and uplifting to the other person, or if you think it will make you feel better without concern for the other person's feelings, you are not ready to make amends. So when do you make amends? When you stop punishing yourself by your continued focus on your character defects, when you stop blaming others, and when you stop complaining about what's wrong with government, the world, big business, religions, and everything else, then you will know if you need to make amends or not. And you will know how and when as well.

Remember, you are a spark of God, so start acting like it.

8

Nurture a Positive Mental Attitude

MY DOMINANT INTENTION EVERY DAY is to feel good. When I find myself in a negative place or in the presence of a negative person or dwelling on my character defects, wallowing in self-pity, criticizing, or blaming someone, I embrace the negative feeling. I give thanks for it, because it lets me know that my emotional guidance system is working perfectly and that my attention is focused in the wrong direction.

Then I pause and reflect, looking for the opposite quality or for a positive and uplifting-feeling thought. I use this as an opportunity to reach for the next best-feeling thought, and I keep reaching for the next best-feeling thought until I am feeling better. For example, if I feel fearful and shaky, I know I feel bad, yet if I feel happy and smiling, I know I feel good. I can easily tell when I feel good or when I feel bad.

I remind myself as often as I can as I go through my day that there is nothing more important than to feel good; everything else flows from that. I jog my memory as I move through the day that I need to focus my thoughts on topics and things that make me feel good.

When I am listening to others, I tell myself, "I value their opinion and I appreciate where they are in their growth because I realize that I cannot change them, nor do I want to, because only they can."

If I make a mistake or insult, injure, or behave rudely to another, I turn my attention to the question "What would have been a wiser thought, statement, or action?"

Every time I speak with others, I no longer use the word *you* when talking to them, but I use the word *I*, which signals that "I no longer have to pretend that I know what's good for another. Rather, I am now taking responsibility for my well-being and I no longer need to give advice to try to build up my self-esteem by pretending I'm smarter than another."

I continually advise myself that well-being is the natural state for me and the very foundation of the universe.

I follow these simple guidelines, combined with following steps ten and eleven according to the directions in this book, and I feel I am well on my way to fostering and nurturing a positive mental attitude and feeling good about myself most of the time.

My objective is to feel good ninety percent of the time every day. Think it's possible? I do.

C H A P T E R

9

How to Do Step Eleven and Feel Good about Yourself

STEP ELEVEN SAYS, "SOUGHT THROUGH prayer and meditation to improve our conscious contact with God as *we understood Him,* praying only for knowledge of His will for us and the power to carry that out."[18] This is a monumental, wonderful step, but the way step eleven describes meditation makes no sense to me.

On the one hand, step eleven gives beautiful directions on how to pray. For example, it says, "We usually conclude the period of meditation with a prayer that we be shown all through the day what our next step is to be, that we be given whatever we need to take care of such problems."[19] On the subject of meditation, however, step eleven offers no clear directions that helped me make conscious contact with God.

For example, step eleven also says, "When we retire at night we constructively review our day. Were we resentful, selfish, dishonest or afraid? Do we owe an apology?"[20]

How do these questions help a person feel good, let alone make conscious contact with God through meditation, when they focus on the negative?

When I learned to meditate, I was taught several spiritual methods, all of which are designed to align one with the Source Energy, with God.

There are many names for God: Almighty, Supreme Being, Allah, Brahma, Ishvara, All That Is, One-without-a-Second, Spirit, Lord, Father, I AM, Source Energy, Yahweh, Most High, Force, Broader Perspective, Inner Being, Great Reality, Higher Power, and so on.

Choose your favorite name according to your religious leanings and use that name when meditating. When you meditate, pick a time of day in the a.m. or p.m. or both, and meditate at that same time every day. Choose a seating posture that is comfortable, but not so comfortable that you will fall asleep. In addition, choose a place in the home where you will not be disturbed by others or by the phone. Wear loose and comfortable clothing so you don't feel restricted.

Now let us look at how to meditate and to apply the name of your chosen deity. Bring your attention to the place where you are sitting. Be aware of yourself. Relax the forehead. Feel the flow and the touch of the breath in your nostrils. Breathe in gently, slowly, normally, and naturally through the nose. Whichever name of the Almighty you chose as your favorite, think that name when exhaling without a break in the breath, and think that name when inhaling without a break in the breath. Breathe normally and naturally without a pause in your breath as you mentally repeat your favorite name of the Almighty on the inhaling and exhaling breath.

If you are an atheist, agnostic, or do not relate to any religious deity, then breathe normally and naturally, feeling the touch of the flow of the breath in the nostrils as you inhale and exhale, always breathing normally and naturally without a pause as you quietly observe your breathing.

If you are attracted to eastern mystical Yoga Sanskrit meditation techniques, then think *Hum* when exhaling without a break in the breath and think *So* when inhaling without a break in the breath. Breathe normally and naturally without a pause in the breath, as you mentally and silently repeat your mantra.

A word phrase in Sanskrit is called a mantra. A mantra is a word or a series of words that have power beyond the ordinary meaning of words. A mantra is a linkage of the lower consciousness with the higher consciousness, which has the capacity of affecting a personality change. The true definition of the mantra is the experience it ultimately creates in the individual consciousness.

If and when you are ready for a personal mantra, remember the saying, "When the student is ready, the teacher will appear." In the meantime, the So-Hum mantra is universal. It is the sound of your breath in Sanskrit and means I Am That.

Step Eleven: Upon Retiring at Night

The following examples are meant to empower you and keep your attention off the negative. The questions and answers I have given are examples of my daily routines. I recommend you get out a piece of paper and change each of these examples and each of the statements to fit you and your situation. Remember, the whole purpose of these questions and answers is to empower you and to evoke a state of feeling good. If my questions and statements don't resonate with you, then make up your own.

- What did I learn today? What did I learn from this situation? What would have been a wiser action?
  Example:
  A person told me, "Next time you come to this AA meeting, leave your ego at the door." I asked, "What do you mean?" The person responded in a negative tone, "You know what I mean." I said, "Sorry, no idea." Indignantly, the person stated, "No one is interested in your drinking story when you lived in Europe and Mexico." I responded angrily, "Sounds like you are having difficulty where I did my drinking and did part of my recovery. Well, that's your problem, not mine." I turned my back to him and walked away abruptly, without offering him another opportunity to speak. Later, when reflecting on this matter, I thought a wiser action would have been to pause and reflect to get myself

into a better feeling space, without any need to correct him, and just walk away.

Take note that all of the following questions and examples are specifically designed to move you in the direction of feeling good. If they don't fit your belief system, create your own answers and statements.

- What do I like about living on this planet?
  Example:
  I love the beauty of the oceans and rivers.
  I love the unlimited growth opportunities.
  I love the limitless opportunities for having fun.
  I love experiencing the contrasts.

- Who and what am I?
  Example:
  I am God, creator of worlds in a physical body.
  I am a Christian who is applying the virtues of Jesus' teachings.
  I am a Hindu practicing the rituals of Krishna.
  I am a Buddhist practicing the teachings of Buddha.
  I am an agnostic or atheist who recognizes my desire for a happy, harmonious, productive life.

- How am I doing?
  Example:
  I am doing just fine.

Everything is unfolding perfectly just as it should for me.

Everything I am experiencing is right on schedule.

- How can my life be better?
  Example:
  Think thoughts that make me feel better.
  Do things that make me feel better.
  Be around people who are positive and uplifting.

- What will come next?
  Example:
  Whatever I choose.

- Now I sit quietly and meditate.

Step Eleven: Upon Awakening

Every day I sit quietly and meditate with the intention of having and maintaining conscious contact with God, because nothing is more significant than my relationship to God. After meditation, I use the following statements, which hold the intention to empower myself and evoke feeling good.

- I love . . .
  Example:
  I love feeling good.
  I love thinking thoughts that make me feel good.

I love going to places that make me feel good.
I love seeing things that make *me* feel good.

- I am in the process of . . .
  Example:
  I am in the process of living an amazing life.
  I'm in the process of consciously expressing God, Source Energy in every area of my life through this body.

- I appreciate . . .
  Example:
  I appreciate I am a *recovered* alcoholic.
  I appreciate I keep my word.
  I appreciate I am open-minded.
  I appreciate all the good that big government and big business do for people.
  I appreciate the unlimited growth opportunities that this life gives me.

- I'm expecting . . .
  Example:
  I'm expecting to master the art and science of feeling good.
  I'm expecting to surround myself with positive, uplifting people.
  I'm expecting to understand and master the law of attraction.

- When I'm in the zone, I feel. (Here I repeat a part of step ten as repetition of these statements helps bring my awareness to an even higher level of feeling good.)

  Example:

  When I am in the zone, I feel elated.

  When I am in the zone, I feel enriched.

  When I am in the zone, I feel yummy.

  When I am in the zone, I feel joyous.

  When I am in the zone, I feel carefree.

  When I am in the zone, I feel happy.

When I direct my thoughts in this manner, I am continually pointing myself in the direction of feeling good, which will eventually get me into the zone. The whole purpose of this repetition and this entire line of thinking is to craft a new thought pattern that will make feeling good a natural way of thinking and living.

Then, I take this feel-good state with me as I go about my day. A typical day for me looks like this: I get up, meditate, review these questions and answers, clean up, take a walk, and go to work as the spiritual director of the Yoga Health Institute, where I mentor yoga teachers on how to deepen their emotional mastery practice. Later in the day, I meet with one of the people I mentor. At some point during the day, I run some errands. Then every night before bed, I meditate and review all the good things about me, life, government, business, and so on.

As I go about my day, I am always reminding myself as often as I can remember that it is my dominant intention to feel good, as everything else flows from that. The theme of my day, no matter what I am doing, where I am going, where I am, or who I am with, always remains the same—to remember to feel good.

C H A P T E R

10

Steps Ten and Eleven: Putting It All Together

U PON AWAKENING, I SIT QUIETLY and meditate with the intention of having and maintaining conscious contact with Source Energy, God, as nothing is more significant than my relationship between me and Source Energy.

During the day, I remind myself I've got only one thing to do and that's to feel good; everything else flows from that. This is so important I cannot repeat myself enough.

Going to bed, I review my day.

I follow steps ten and eleven in this new way and watch the changes that take place in my attitude and behavior.

Remember, negative thoughts and negative feelings attract more negative thoughts and negative circumstances, and happy thoughts and happy feelings invite more happy thoughts and happy situations.

I designed steps ten and eleven to help me think happy thoughts and feel happy feelings, which would also help me to get in the zone. Feedback from the people I mentored has confirmed this effect. One of the people I mentor, Vickie, told me, "By applying the steps as you taught me, I found that not only did I start to feel better, but I also noticed from time to time a subtle shift toward experiencing deeper feelings of what I describe as delightful and delicious. When I experience this deeper level, I want to cry because I never felt anything like this before in my life."[21]

I found that all it takes is practice and a willingness to do the work. It's like building a new muscle—it takes time, but once I got my momentum, it became easy and fun.

After exercising my new mental muscle for three months by doing steps ten and eleven the way I explained in a previous chapter, I realized I had built the new thought pattern I needed to feel good and to get into the zone. As a result, I streamlined the two steps and put them in this format.

Once comfortable doing the steps as outlined in previous chapters, follow the new streamlined version for maximum benefit as outlined below.

Step Eleven: In the Morning or Upon Awakening

- Meditate for two minutes. Increase the time to twenty minutes over the next six months.
- State my dominant intention: "I've got only one thing to do today and that's to feel good, to please

me, to be good to me; everything else flows from that."

- Answer the question: What do I appreciate about me?
- Plan my day and include something fun to do.

Step Ten: During the Day

- A reminder: "I've got only one thing to do today and that's to feel good, to please me, to be good to me; everything else flows from that."
- When stuck or negative, reach for the next best-feeling thought.
- Remember to smile.

Step Eleven: In the Evening, or Before Bedtime

Meditate for two minutes, but first answer these questions:

- What's good about me?
- What's good about life?
- What do I want my future to look and feel like?

Remember, happy thoughts and happy feelings summon happy situations. If you'll let the journey of reaching for the next best-feeling thought be your goal, then you will experience instant success by continually reaching for the next best-feeling thought. Achieving your goal of feeling good is guaranteed.

CHAPTER

11

What Is a Spiritual Awakening?

WHAT IS A SPIRITUAL AWAKENING? Is it a ball of light exploding inside you, which offers indescribable joy without the need for outside stimuli? To me this is a spiritual experience. Others may interpret this as an awakening.

I had a spiritual experience that was like a blazing white light exploding inside me without warning. I now know that this set me on the path of personal and spiritual growth.

I believe a spiritual awakening is a process, during which my personality, my attitudes, my ideas, and my behaviors changed for the better over time. My old ideas, thoughts, and actions have been cast aside. A new person has emerged, a new me I continue to nourish with steps ten and eleven as written in this book.

I remember a time when I was argumentative and defensive. I had to win any argument at all costs. Recently, a close friend of mine, Hank, disagreed with my point of view and started to argue with me to prove his point. I diffused the argument simply by saying, "You're right." He responded, "What did you say?" I said, "You're right." He just sat there with his mouth open with nothing more to say. The moral of the story: Would you rather be right or happy?

Over time, I became more positive in thought, attitude, and behavior. Most often, I express myself in positive, healthy, and uplifting ways. My overall state of mind exhibits emotional sobriety by respecting myself and others, as well as feeling good about myself most of the time.

When presenting my concept of emotional sobriety to people I mentor, friends, acquaintances, coworkers, or strangers, I explain that it is based upon my life experiences, my current beliefs, my emotional responses to people, places, and events, and on my understanding of the twelve steps of AA, in particular my reinterpretation of steps ten and eleven. Over time, I have grown, and so has my understanding of how to help other people whether they are alcoholics or not. I have found that everyone can use steps ten and eleven as I have rewritten them.

I believe the best mentors are emotionally healthy. They teach by example and are ready to mentor anyone who asks for help. I believe it is more important to set the example of a happy, joyous, and free person's thoughts, comments, and actions and let that be the attraction rather than to seek out someone and try to convince them to do steps ten and eleven as I have explained. I have found that people have sought me out because they were being drawn to me just by who and what I am.

Experience has taught me that when a person is ready to take the next step toward self-improvement, the right mentor who will match their current level of understanding will be there to help them. For example, when I made up my mind to make and maintain conscious contact with God, I was unexpectedly invited to India by Swami Veda to do a forty-day silent retreat in the Himalayan Mountains. There I was given a personal mantra to assist me in making conscious contact with Source Energy, God.

When I started to expand my understanding for self-improvement by doing steps ten and eleven in the way I describe, I found that I grew in two directions simultaneously. One, internally, toward my Eternal Self where I believe there is never-ending joy and freedom bubbling up inside without any outside stimuli. Two, externally, toward developing mastery of the external world that is full of confusion, competiveness, and temporary happiness and joy, which depends on outside objects for fulfillment. Not that I don't enjoy outside pleasures. I do, yet I kept falling into the trap of dependency, and could never find enough things to consistently do or have that would fill that empty hole that I so often tried to fill with alcohol, drugs, sex, and international travel.

To sum up, it's your choice to step into the leading edge of thought to grow and change in healthy, productive ways and feel good about yourself. Alternately, you can choose to remain stuck feeling bad as you continue to give attention to your character defects, to what's wrong with other people and about the world. The choice is yours.

This information is easy to apply; all it takes is your willingness to practice.

Let whatever experiences come your way be your experience. Don't compare them to mine or anyone else's. Honor yourself.

CHAPTER

12

What's the *Number One* Secret to Feeling Good?

I HAVE FOUND THAT THE *number one* secret to feeling good is the following statement of my dominant intention: "I've got only one thing to do today and that's to feel good, to please me, to be good to me; everything else flows from that."

When I say this, I start feeling good within. Throughout the day I continue to use this as a guiding principle for my thoughts, emotions, and actions. I remind myself that this is my dominant intention, regardless of what I am doing, where I am, where I'm going, or who I am with.

Let me give you an example of how this dominant intention translates into my relationships. No matter who I am with, I remind myself that my intention in this relationship is to feel good, to please me, and to be good to me. I tell myself that it is also my sincere hope that the other person is doing the same. From that intention, I have noticed I have attracted people to me who like feeling good, who do things that please them and make them feel good. When I am in their presence, we both tend to feel good, yet we don't feel dependent on the other for our well-being. It's very exhilarating to be in this kind of relationship.

My experience tells me that the secret to feeling good is making feeling good my dominant intention, along with being good to me and pleasing me. Because my experience has shown me that every time I think a thought to feel good or to be good to me, I move in the right direction and become aligned with God, Source Energy, All That Is—a place of immense internal joy that bubbles up endlessly from within.

"Let your desire for pleasure—your desire for feeling good—be your only guiding light. As you seek those thoughts that feel good, you will always be in vibrational harmony with the Energy that is your Source. And under those conditions, only good can come to you, and only good can come from you."[22]

To help myself to practice feeling good while simultaneously getting into the zone, I follow the information in the book and use the tools provided in the chapters that help me to implement the outline and align myself with Source Energy, God, All That Is.

Don't believe me because I tell you it will work; do the work as outlined in this book and prove to yourself that you too can feel good, no matter what you are going through or what is going on your life.

Recently, I had a new cancer scare and needed a biopsy. Between the time of the biopsy and the results, I saw myself starting down that old familiar path of fear and worry. I was doing what I had done before: I was beating myself up with the club of fear. I disregarded everything I had learned about feeling good and the growth I had experienced.

Then after about two weeks of wallowing in self-pity, I reminded myself that I had created ways for me to feel good, and that this was a great time to practice what I preach. I realized that to feel good when things are going well is easy, but what about when I am in a difficult situation?

I started to tell myself a new story in order to find some relief and move in the direction of feeling good.

"I believe that wellness is my natural state. Where I am right now in my situation, I'm glad I don't have to figure everything out this minute. I feel a little lost, but I feel I have some flexibility in this. I have a sense that the way I'm thinking and feeling needs to be changed. While I can't figure out exactly what to do or how to align with feeling good and my wellness in this moment, I can feel that ease is a better path toward health, and that getting in the zone is a better way to align myself with my well-being than beating the drum of being afraid and worrying about the results of the biopsy. The results will be what they will be, and I can't control that. Thinking like this is starting to make me feel better, because I believe that the natural state of me is one of well-being. And I like feeling well. In fact, it's fun.

Okay, now I'm moving in the right direction. I'm starting to feel a little better. Turning toward feeling better is enough for me right now. Not only is that enough, it's all I feel I can do. I am at peace with that. What I want may be a bit in the future, but I am now pointed in the right direction. And now that I'm pointed in the right direction, I'm feeling some relief right this minute. I so appreciate the health I have. I feel blessed with my current health, and I'm looking forward to my health improving every day, day by day. Thank you, God."

I read this story out loud two or three times a day. Then, after I read it, I would ask empowering questions: What's good about this? How can I grow from this? The essence of my story and the questions gave me some relief and got me back on track to feeling good.

Within two weeks I started feeling better, and another week later I felt so much better that I forgot about the results of the biopsy. I decided that if it was cancer, I would let it run its course, let myself experience the process, let myself die and go into the zone permanently. I not only felt relief, but feeling good became easier every time the thought of being sick with cancer came into my mind.

The results arrived. The biopsy was negative.

Remember, feeling good does not absolve you from being responsible for yourself and for those in your charge or from being a productive member (whatever that means) of society, unless of course you choose to be a hermit, a mountain man, a vagabond, a gypsy, a world traveler, a nun, a monk, or something of the sort.

You have the power to choose to feel good. Make that choice today and use the methods in this book. Most people

I have talked to and met, including myself, have only wanted the pain to stop for most of their lives, never realizing that it was okay to feel good. I mean really, really, really feel good.

The whole idea of being *recovered* is to push the button of feeling good as often as possible and to discover the zone within. You have the control to shape your destiny by the simple concept of feeling good, no matter if you are an alcoholic or not. Feeling good applies to all of us.

"The only person you are destined to become is the person you decide to be."[23]

Appendix:
Twelve Steps of Alcoholics Anonymous

Alcoholics Anonymous, fourth edition,
New and Revised, 2001

1. We admitted we were powerless over alcohol that our lives had become unmanageable.
2. Came to believe that a Power greater than ourselves could restore us to sanity.
3. Made a decision to turn our will and our lives over to the care of God *as we understood Him.*
4. Made a searching and fearless moral inventory of ourselves.
5. Admitted to God, to ourselves, and to another human being the exact nature of our wrongs.
6. Were entirely ready to have God remove all these defects of character.
7. Humbly asked Him to remove our shortcomings.
8. Made a list of all persons we had harmed, and became willing to make amends to them all.

9. Made direct amends to such people wherever possible, except when do so would injure them or others.

10. Continued to take personal inventory and when we were wrong promptly admitted it.

11. Sought through prayer and meditation to improve our conscious contact with God *as we understood Him,* praying only for knowledge of His will for us and the power to carry that out.

12. Having had a spiritual awakening as the result of these steps, we tried to carry this message to alcoholics, and to practice these principles in all our affairs.

Endnotes

Introduction

1. *Alcoholics Anonymous*, fourth edition, New and Revised (2001), 59, 60.

Chapter 1

2. *Alcoholics Anonymous*, fourth edition, New and Revised (2001), 59.
3. Ibid., 84.
4. Ibid., 59.
5. Ibid., 86.
6. Ibid., 20.
7. Jack and Richard sitting in a sidewalk café having coffee in Modesto, California, July 2008.
8. Jane and Richard visiting in San Francisco, California, March 2009.
9. Paul and Richard having lunch in Modesto, California, February 2010.
10. Gertrude and Richard sitting in a sidewalk café in San Francisco, California, June 3, 2012.

Chapter 3

11. *Alcoholics Anonymous*, fourth edition, New and Revised (2001), 133.
12. Bill Wilson, "The Next Frontier: Emotional Sobriety," *Grapevine Magazine*, (1958).
13. Ibid.

Chapter 4

14. Larry and Richard visiting in Modesto, California, August 2013.

Chapter 5

15. Ellen Grace Obrien (spiritual director, Center for Spiritual Enlightenment), Email Quote of the Day, June 2013.

Chapter 7

16. *Alcoholics Anonymous*, fourth edition, New and Revised (2001), 59.
17. Ibid., 59.

Chapter 9

18. *Alcoholics Anonymous*, fourth edition, New and Revised (2001), 59.
19. Ibid., 87.
20. Ibid., 86.

Chapter 10

21. Vickie and Richard having lunch in Sausalito, California, November 2012.

Chapter 12

22. Abraham-Hicks, excerpted from the workshop in Philadelphia, April 14, 1998.
23. Ralph Waldo Emerson, American poet, essayist, lecturer. Born: May 25, 1803. Died: April 27, 1887.